21st Century Skills Library

GLOBAL PRODUCTS

INTERACTIVE WHITEBOARDS

John Matthews

Cherry Lake Publishing
Ann Arbor, Michigan

Published in the United States of America by Cherry Lake Publishing
Ann Arbor, Michigan
www.cherrylakepublishing.com

Content Adviser: Kimberly Quinn-Hutchinson, Director Education Business Development, PolyVision Corporation

Photo Credits: Cover and pages 1, 20, and 23, Photo courtesy of PolyVision; page 4, ©Stephen Aaron Rees, used under license from Shutterstock, Inc.; page 6, ©Glow Images/Alamy; page 9, ©Stefan Glebowski, used under license from Shutterstock, Inc.; page 10, ©AP Photo/Michael Schmelling; page 13, ©graham tomlin, used under license from Shutterstock, Inc.; page 14, ©AP Photo/Stuart Ramson; page 16, ©Patrick Eden/Alamy; page 18, ©Trevor Smith/Alamy; page 19, ©Zak Waters/Alamy; page 22, ©Nicola Armstrong/Alamy; page 24, ©Mark Dyball/ Alamy; page 26, ©Opla, used under license from Shutterstock, Inc.

Map by XNR Productions Inc.

Library of Congress Cataloging-in-Publication Data
Matthews, John, 1945–
Interactive whiteboards / by John Matthews.
p. cm.—(Global products)
Includes index.
ISBN-13: 978-1-60279-254-8
ISBN-10: 1-60279-254-2
1. Interactive whiteboards—Juvenile literature. 2. Teaching—Aids and devices—Juvenile literature. 3. Education, Elementary—Audio-visual aids—Juvenile literature. I. Title. II. Series.
LB1043.5.M35 2009
371.33'4—dc22 2008003904

Cherry Lake Publishing would like to acknowledge the work of The Partnership for 21st Century Skills. Please visit www.21stcenturyskills.org *for more information.*

Table of Contents

CHAPTER ONE

Field Trip to Beaverton

Chalkboards were used in classrooms for many years. Today, many are being replaced by interactive whiteboards.

Ms. Brennan herded her sixth-grade class into the conference room at PolyVision's manufacturing plant in Beaverton, Oregon. PolyVision makes **interactive** whiteboards.

"What makes whiteboards interactive?" Jeremy asked.

"How does the computer know what you're writing on the whiteboard?" Laura asked.

"Kids," said Ms. Brennan, "this is Mr. Hill. He's going to tell us about interactive whiteboards. By the time we leave, he will have answered all your questions."

Mr. Hill walked to the front of the room. Using his finger, he wrote his name on the interactive whiteboard. He touched the color icon on the **toolbar** on the side of the board. He touched the red icon, then wrote his name again—this time in red.

"Wow," Jeremy said. "I've always wondered how that works."

"Maybe today you'll find out," said Laura.

Ms. Brennan remembered her many years as a teacher. "Before whiteboards were interactive, they were simple white metal boards that you wrote on with grease pencils. These metal boards had replaced chalkboards in classrooms and conference rooms. Just like chalk, the multicolored grease pencils could easily be wiped clean from the whiteboard. Today, Mr. Hill is going to help us understand how we got from simple metal boards to the interactive whiteboards used today."

■ ■ ■

Whiteboards replaced chalkboards long before people had the idea to make them interactive. The first noninteractive whiteboards were

MIT is one of several institutions that played a role in the development of interactive whiteboard technology.

made of glass that was painted white on the back side and written on with grease pencils. Other whiteboards were made from glass-coated steel. These boards could have notes attached to them using magnets.

The ideas that led to interactive whiteboards were explored at the University of Toronto, AT&T, Massachusetts Institute of Technology (MIT), and Palo Alto Research Center (PARC) in California. Researchers explored ways to save notes written on the whiteboard to a computer file. They explored ways that a computer could be controlled from a whiteboard and made to display text and graphics on the board.

Like many inventions, interactive whiteboards used existing technology in new ways. Technology that made computer monitors sensitive to touch and that would make whiteboards interactive was already widely used. It was used in automatic teller machines (ATMs) as well as information systems in stores.

SMART Technologies introduced the first commercially available interactive whiteboard in 1991. The company's **touch-sensitive** whiteboard was connected to a computer and a **projector** that projected the computer screen onto the whiteboard.

Competitors recognized the importance of the interactive whiteboard idea and entered the market with products of their own. A new global industry was born. Interactive whiteboards are now used around the world. Manufacturers have introduced **innovations** and variations to the technology. They have also developed other equipment that can be used with interactive whiteboards.

PolyVision, for example, has developed the TS Series interactive whiteboards, which are driven by Webster software and controlled by the **icon strip** on the boards. The ability to control the computer from the whiteboard means that any software that will work in the computer will work on the whiteboard. Webster software allows users to mark up or highlight text. Lessons can be saved and replayed for review. PolyVision's Walk-and-Talk interactive whiteboards are controlled by remote control.

Interactive whiteboards can also be used with **Web conferencing** software to connect two or more computers over the Internet. Businesses with multiple locations can eliminate travel by using the technology for business meetings. This saves the company both time and money. Web conferencing technology can also be used by schools for **distance learning**.

21st Century Content

PolyVision Corporation is a global company that has been in business since 1954. It produced whiteboards long before they became interactive. All PolyVision products sold in the United States are made in either Oregon, California, Oklahoma, or Pennsylvania. Products sold to its overseas market are manufactured in Belgium, Denmark, and France.

PolyVision has **patents** for laser-based whiteboards, meeting room signage, whiteboard erasers, camera systems for capturing whiteboards, and remote meeting technologies. Like other interactive whiteboard manufacturers, this company continues to come up with new ideas for improving whiteboards. Their development teams are always looking for new ideas that will allow people in different locations to work together more easily. Coming up with new ideas is a must for any company that wants to stay competitive in today's global marketplace.

CHAPTER TWO

The Touch Screen

A mouse is a type of pointing device.

"We've learned that the interactive whiteboard works when you touch it with your finger or a marker," Mr. Hill said. "Who would imagine that the mouse may have inspired the invention of touch-sensitive technology?"

"I would imagine it," Jeremy said.

"You would not," Laura shot back.

Hector interjected, "You mean the computer mouse, don't you Mr. Hill?"

Douglas Engelbart, the inventor of the computer mouse, holds the one he designed in the 1960s.

"Yes. Let's take a look at how touch screens were invented. We'll start with the mouse, sometimes referred to as a pointing device."

■ ■ ■

Older computers needed only a keyboard and monitor to operate. When computers that display graphics such as pictures and icons were created, some kind of pointing device was needed. Icons are the symbols on the monitor that open programs when the mouse, or pointing device, is moved over them and clicked.

In 1964, Douglas Engelbart, a scientist at Stanford University, made the first computer mouse. It was nicknamed "mouse" because the wire coming out the back looked like a mouse tail. That first mouse was a small wooden box with two metal wheels. Engelbart received a patent for his invention in 1970. His patent application described the mouse as an "x-y position indicator for a display system." The "x-y position" refers to intersecting points on a graph. A computer monitor is one kind of display system.

The first public appearance of the mouse was at a demonstration held in 1968. The mouse made possible the use of the Windows Display System, sometimes referred to as a **graphical user interface** (GUI).

David Thornburg first thought of a touch-sensitive pointing device as an alternative to the mouse while working at the Xerox Corporation in the 1970s. His touch-tablet idea was this: Two sheets coated with a special material were placed against each other, with a small air gap between them. The bottom sheet would have **electrodes** at the left and right edges. The top sheet would have electrodes at the top and bottom edges. When voltage was applied to the electrodes, the x-y coordinates, or intersecting

Life & Career Skills

Douglas Engelbart changed the way computers worked. Besides inventing the mouse, he contributed to other computer technology, including Windows, e-mail, and the Internet. In 1998, he was inducted into the National Inventors Hall of Fame.

Engelbart was an electronics technician in the U.S. Navy during World War II. He earned a bachelor's degree and worked at NASA's Ames Research Laboratory. He went on to earn his doctorate from the University of California at Berkeley. Like many inventors, he understood the importance of continually advancing his skill levels and expanding his knowledge.

points, would be located wherever the sheets were touched. That is similar to the way a mouse works. Thornburg built a touch screen and placed it over a computer monitor. He used the touch screen instead of a mouse to operate the computer.

Thornburg made a distinction between touch tablets and touch screens. Tablets are used on horizontal surfaces such as the touch pad on a notebook computer. Touch screens are used on vertical surfaces such as computer monitors and interactive whiteboards.

PolyVision's TS Series interactive whiteboards are made interactive using technology similar to Thornburg's. PolyVision developed the process for using the technology on large surfaces.

How are interactive whiteboards made? A thin sheet of polyester plastic material, called the bottom sheet, is attached directly to the front surface of the board. Another thin sheet of polyester plastic, called the top sheet, is stretched over the board. This creates a tiny space between the sheets, called the gap. Each sheet is coated with a film that allows a small electrical current to flow through it. The pressure from marking on the board causes the two sheets to come into contact with each other. These markings can then be captured by the computer.

Other technologies are sometimes used to make whiteboards interactive. Some whiteboards are wired with **electromagnetic** sensors.

Many personal digital assistants (PDAs) work by responding to the touch of a stylus.

They react when touched by a stylus, or magnetic pen. Others use wires that are sensitive to fingers touching the screen. Still others use a combination of infrared lights and ultrasonic waves.

The whiteboard is only one part of interactive whiteboard technology. Software, computers, and projectors are also needed. Teachers use interactive whiteboards with a variety of software for lessons in many different subjects such as math, social studies, literature, and science. Businesses use interactive whiteboards along with software especially designed for that company's products and services.

CHAPTER THREE

Keep Your Eyes on the Whiteboard

A woman demonstrates how to use an interactive whiteboard made by Smart Technologies at a trade show in 2003.

Ms. Brennan looked at Jeremy as the class filed out of the conference room on the way to lunch. "Have you learned anything yet, Jeremy?"

"I learned why it's important to understand how to find x and y points on a graph," he replied. "Now I know why you keep telling us that math is so important—it's everywhere!"

■ ■ ■

PolyVision manufactures its whiteboards both in the United States and in Europe. SMART Technologies manufactures most of its whiteboards in

Canada. It exports whiteboards to the United States as well as to European countries. There are many companies around the world, especially in Asia, that manufacture whiteboards and sell them in the United States.

China has more than 20 interactive whiteboard manufacturers. One, Julong Educational Technology, is located in Shenzhen, in China's industrial region north of Hong Kong. It was founded in 1995 by Chinese investment companies and other investors from around the world. Its products are shipped to Europe, Asia, Africa, North America, and South America. Its sales company in the United States is Invision Power Services, located in Forest, Virginia. Invision sells Julong's IP Board in the American market.

There are many other similar companies in China and Taiwan. These companies supply interactive whiteboards that many companies in the United States, such as Hitachi, sell under their own brand names.

Learning & Innovation Skills

A wireless slate is an interactive whiteboard small enough for a student desk or table. It connects with and can control the large class whiteboard using a mouse or pen. It allows students to participate in whiteboard activities from their desks.

Can you think of some ways that wireless slates would be useful in your classroom?

CHAPTER FOUR

USING THE WHITEBOARD

A student works on a math problem on an interactive whiteboard in a classroom in England.

Ms. Brennan's class returned to the conference room after lunch to wait for Mr. Hill to continue the tour. She asked the class some questions as they waited. "Laura, have you learned anything so far?"

"Yes," she replied. "I learned that there are lots of companies around the world that make interactive whiteboards."

"Very good, Laura. The interactive whiteboard is a good example of a global product. One of the most important things we've learned during our tour is not about the boards themselves. It is how teachers and businesses all over the world are using them."

A new visitor entered the room. Mr. Anders was a businessman from Montreal, Canada. While waiting for Mr. Hill, he joined the discussion. "I'm a corporate trainer. That's a little bit like being a schoolteacher. I train employees in many different countries. I hope interactive whiteboards can help us overcome some communication problems, especially language barriers."

Mr. Hill returned and invited Mr. Anders to come along on the tour. "Ms. Brennan, does your school have particular requirements for selecting a product?" asked Mr. Hill.

"Yes," she replied. "It has to be easy to operate or teachers won't use it. It has to be priced right or the school board won't buy it."

"Let me tell you about a school in Leicestershire, England, that is using PolyVision's TS Series interactive whiteboards. They had several requirements like yours. The Webster software is simple to use. They trained their teachers quickly and easily. The whole system had to be sturdy enough to withstand constant use. It had to support the full range of educational software and online resources. They're happy with the boards."

"That sounds like what we're looking for," Ms. Brennan said.

■ ■ ■

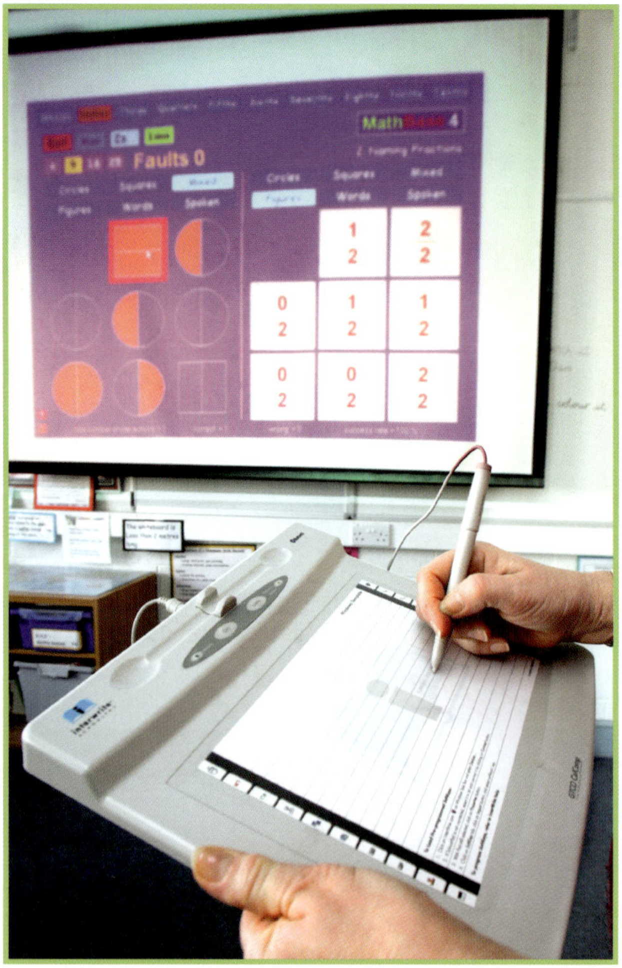

A math teacher presents a lesson using a wireless slate linked to an interactive whiteboard.

Whiteboard interactivity can be both local and global. Business training was the first use targeted by developers of interactive whiteboards. Now many schools use them. In classes where students each have a wireless slate, teachers can interact with individual students. They can evaluate learning without having to pass out worksheets or tests and then wait for papers to be graded before responding to students.

A student highlights text on an interactive whiteboard.

School lesson software is available for a variety of subjects including math, language, history, social studies, and computer instruction. Some computer programs such as Microsoft PowerPoint, developed for business presentations, are useful for both business and classroom lessons. Other programs, such as CorelDRAW and Photoshop, can be used in art class. Art is especially suitable for the boards. Students can be more creative using their fingers or a pen to draw on the board than using a computer mouse. There are also programs developed for teaching music that can work with interactive whiteboards. Apple computer has a music application called GarageBand that allows students to play and compose music using the piano keyboard on whiteboards sized to fit their hands.

Students can interact with each other and even with students in another classroom. No matter what the subject, students can test

A teacher calls on a student to answer a problem on an interactive whiteboard made by PolyVision. PolyVision's headquarters are in the United States.

themselves in real time. Teachers can save class sessions, including student questions and responses. Saved class sessions can be important for evaluating progress. Sessions can be repeated and compared with earlier sessions. Students can pace themselves according to learning ability and can revisit sessions they missed or did not understand.

One leading software company in the United Kingdom, RM Software, produces lessons that cover a wide range of subjects for grades K–12. Their Easiteach software includes a math toolbar that can instantly create number lines, graphs, fractions, symbols, and a compass.

Learning games for interactive whiteboard use also have been developed. For example, the British Broadcasting Company (BBC) television network in the United Kingdom has a science learning game for ages 5 and 6 called "Growing Plants." The lesson shows a plant's growth over a four-week period. A colorful animation invites students to water the plant. A student pushes a button on the animation labeled "grow." The animation shows the water level falling as the plant grows. As the process is repeated, the plant grows to full height. The animation then demonstrates what happens if the plant is not watered. It dies. The lesson is followed by a quiz. Each lesson includes teacher resources and lesson plans. These lessons can be accessed directly from the Internet and are free of charge. Other subjects covered include art, languages, music, and math.

Learning & Innovation Skills

Some lessons for use with interactive whiteboards can be bought ready to use from the interactive whiteboard supplier. Lessons can also be developed by individuals. They can be saved for use in coming years and can be traded with others. Teacher-developed content can come from many sources, including the Internet and libraries.

Do you think you could write a lesson for the interactive whiteboard? What skills do you think you would need to create your lesson plan?

Companies that develop interactive whiteboard software for schools are beginning to compete with companies that produce textbooks. In the future, some schools may even choose to replace some textbooks with interactive whiteboard lessons.

Teachers can develop their own lessons for use on an interactive whiteboard. They can also purchase lessons or use those that are available on the Internet.

CHAPTER FIVE

THE FUTURE OF THE WHITEBOARD

Interactive whiteboards aren't just used in elementary school classrooms. They are also used by university professors.

Ms. Brennan thanked Mr. Hill for the tour of the PolyVision plant. "My students have been very attentive today. That means they were interested in what they were learning. Before we leave, can you tell us a little bit about how interactive whiteboard technology will change in the future?"

Business professionals use headphones to hear language translations of a speaker's presentation. Several companies are developing computer systems that can translate speech.

Mr. Anders said, "I'd like to hear about that, too. When I told a co-worker I was coming to the PolyVision plant, she asked me to find out about new developments, especially new software, and what we could expect for the future. When I have Web conferences and everyone can't speak the same language, I have to provide **interpreters**."

"I think there may be a solution coming for your language problem," said Ms. Brennan. "I remember reading an article that said IBM is developing new software for instant spoken translation. It will eventually be **compatible** with interactive whiteboards."

■ ■ ■

IBM is developing software that will allow a meeting leader or a classroom teacher to speak into a microphone attached to a computer. The computer will instantly **translate** the speaker's words into another language. This software is now called the Multilingual Automatic Speech-to-Speech Translator, or MASTOR. IBM is still working on this project. One of the goals for this software is to have it available for use on **conference calls** or at meetings.

Another emerging technology for interactive whiteboards uses three-dimensional imaging software. Three-dimensional technology is useful for studying the parts of a cell, layers of Earth, fractions, ratios, proportions, and hundreds of other subjects. This is one of the exciting new developments that will be a big part of the future for interactive whiteboards.

A new product called eBeam Projection can turn a blank wall into an interactive whiteboard. It is compact and portable, weighing less than a

Containerships carry goods across the world's oceans.

pound. Its interactive stylus behaves like a mouse. It has right-click and left-click functions and a button for accessing on-screen tools. It is also less expensive than many conventional whiteboard systems.

One thing is certain. Companies developing interactive whiteboard technology will continue to sell their products throughout the world. Some will be shipped from one country to another using cargo ships, airplanes, trucks, and other traditional forms of distribution for goods. Some of the software components will be sold and delivered via the Internet. Customers will be able to download some products within minutes of purchase. Interactive whiteboards are just one more modern product that seems to make distances between countries shrink every day.

■ ■ ■

The sixth-graders were impressed by their one-day introduction to the global impact of interactive whiteboards. As they boarded the bus to return to school, Ms. Brennan addressed the class. "Tomorrow, there will be a test on what we learned today. Count on it."

Learning & Innovation Skills

Multimedia Research Laboratories, a company in Japan, is working on a system that will translate Japanese to English and English to Japanese just as a live interpreter would do. The system will utilize computer software, and users will have their speech translated instantly. Can you describe ways a system such as this could be used with an interactive whiteboard?

This map shows the countries and cities mentioned in the text.

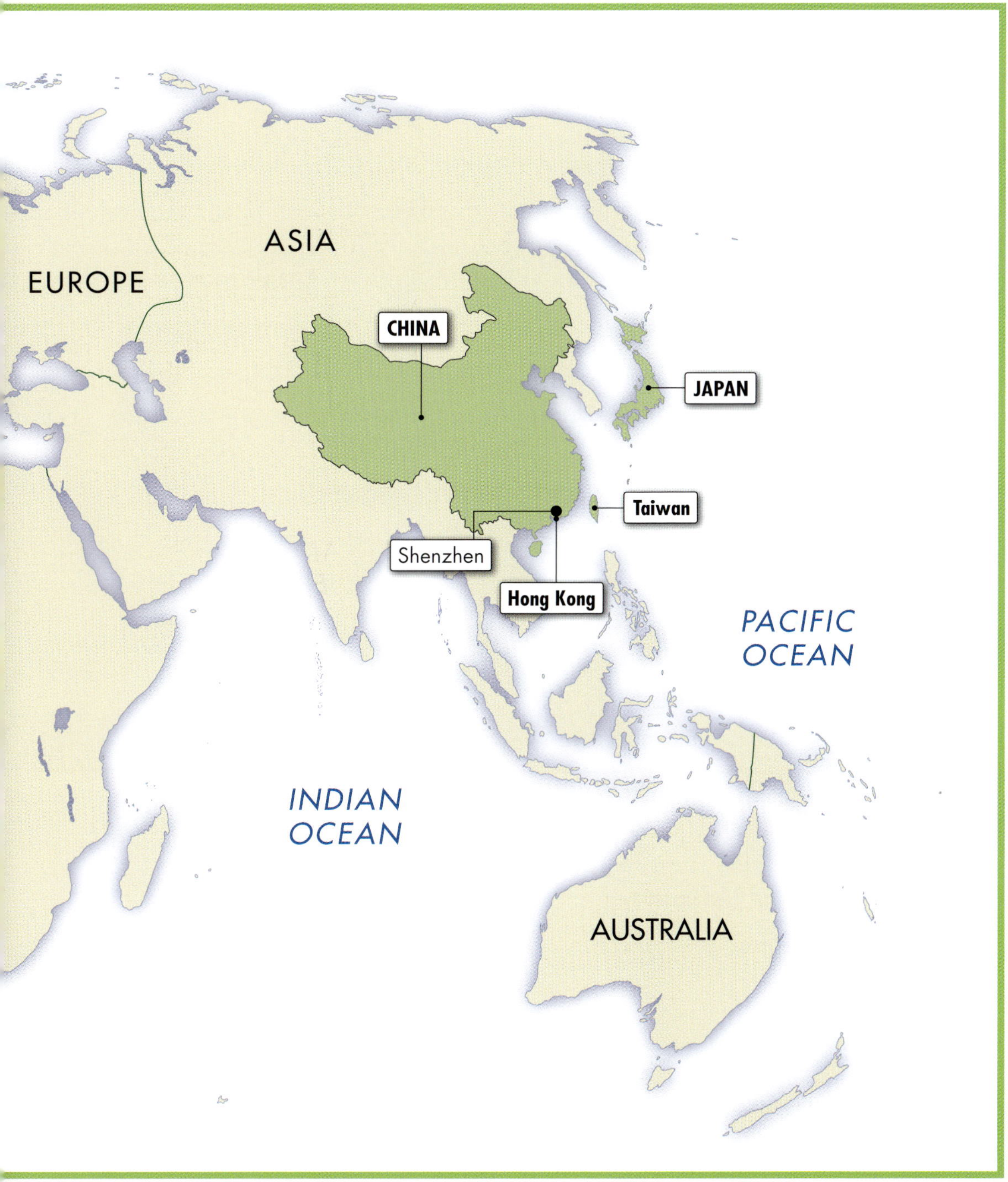

They are the locations of some of the companies involved in the making and selling of interactive whiteboards.

Glossary

compatible (kuhm-PAT-uh-buhl) able to work together

conference calls (KON-fur-uhnss KALLZ) telephone conversations among several people

distance learning (DISS-tuhnss LURN-ing) class in which students can participate by telephone or computer connection

electrodes (ih-LEK-trohdz) conductors, such as wires or plates, through which electricity is passed

electromagnetic (i-lek-troh-mag-NEH-tick) relating to a temporary magnet created by running electricity through a wire coil

graphical user interface (GRAF-ik-uhl YOOZ-uhr IN-tur-fayss) type of computer display that uses pictures and icons to represent programs

icon strip (EYE-kon STRIP) on an interactive whiteboard, touch-sensitive symbols used to control the computer

innovations (in-uh-VAY-shuhnz) changes or improvements to existing technology

interactive (in-tur-AK-tiv) actions that produce a response, such as touching the print symbol on an interactive whiteboard activates the printer

interpreters (in-TUR-prit-urz) people who translate speech from one language into another

patents (PAT-uhnts) rights granted by government to inventors that allow them to control the manufacture and sale of their inventions

projector (pruh-JEK-tur) a machine that displays images onto a screen, such as a movie projector

toolbar (TOOL-bar) icons along the top or bottom of a computer screen that open or control programs

touch-sensitive (TUHCH-SEN-suh-tiv) able to respond to touch, as a whiteboard or computer screen

translate (TRANSS-late) to turn text written or spoken in one language into another

Web conferencing (WEB KON-fruhnss-eng) conducting a meeting in which people in different locations communicate using the Internet

For More Information

Books

Ward-Johnson, Chris, and William Gould. *The Magic Mouse Dictionary of Computers and Information Technology*. Berkeley Heights, NJ: Enslow Elementary, 2003.

Woodford, Chris. *Digital Technology*. New York: Chelsea House, 2006.

Web Sites

Amphitheater Public Schools—Interactive Whiteboard Resources
www.amphi.com/departments/technology/whiteboard/lessonplans.html
Links to interactive whiteboard lessons for all grade levels

Johnny Chung Lee
www.cs.cmu.edu/~johnny/projects/wii/
A demonstration of how to turn a blank wall into an interactive whiteboard using a Wii remote control

PolyVision
www.polyvision.com
Learn more about interactive whiteboards and their uses

Index

About the Author

John Matthews began a new career as an author after a career as a book publisher. He has written numerous books about inventions, wildlife, and history. "The interactive whiteboard has become an essential tool for both schools and businesses," he says. "I wish when I was growing up in Texas, our school could have used interactive whiteboards to share lessons with students in other countries."